5 OF THE BEST
for guitar
METALLICA
Vol. 2

T0078976

Contents

Management: Q Prime, Inc.
Music Engraving by W.R. Music
Production Manager: Daniel Rosenbaum
Art Direction: Rosemary Cappa
Director Of Music: Mark Phillips

Photography by Ross Halfin

Enter Sandman
from "Metallica"

Words and Music by
James Hetfield, Lars Ulrich
and Kirk Hammett

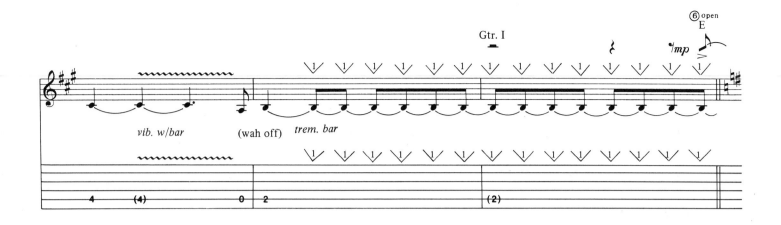

vib. w/bar   (wah off)   trem. bar

w/Riff A (7 times)
N.C.

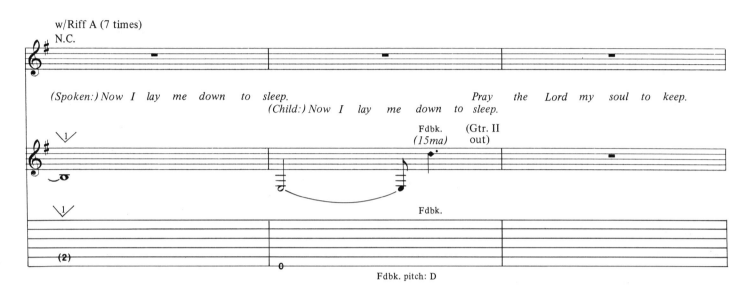

(Spoken:) Now I lay me down to sleep.   *Pray the Lord my soul to keep.*
(Child:) Now I lay me down to sleep.

Fdbk. pitch: D

If I die before I wake,   *pray*
Pray the Lord my soul to keep.   *If I die before I wake,*

w/Rhy. Fill 4

the Lord my soul to take.
pray the Lord my soul to take.

Sad But True
from "Metallica"

Words and Music by
James Hetfield and Lars Ulrich

...And Justice For All
from "...And Justice For All"

Words and Music by
James Hetfield, Lars Ulrich
and Kirk Hammett

1st, 2nd, 3rd Verses
w/Rhy. Fig. 2 *(2 times)*

1. Halls of jus - tice paint - ed green. Mon - ey talk - ing.___
2. Ap - a - thy their step - ping - stone. So un - feel - ing.___
3. La - dy jus - tice has been raped. Truth as - sas - sin.___

Pow - er wolves be - set your door, hear them stalk - ing.
Hid - den deep an - i - mos - i - ty, so de - ceiv - ing.
Rolls of red tape seal your lips. Now your done in.

Soon you'll please their ap - pe - tite, they de - vour.___
Through your eyes their light burns, hop - ing to find.___
Their mon - ey tips her scales a - gain. Make your deal.___

Ham - mer of jus - tice crush - es you. O - ver - pow - er.
In - qui - si - tion seek - ing you with cry - ing ___ might.
Just what is truth? I can - not tell, can - not feel. ___

The ul - ti - mate in van - i - ty. ___

Ex - ploit - ing their ___ su - prem -

Rhy. Fill 1

Rhy. Fill 2

*Vocal rests for two bars.

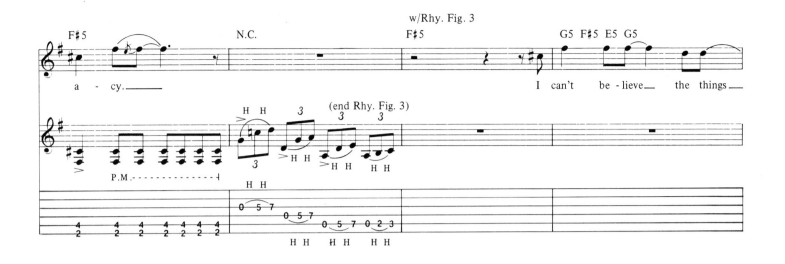

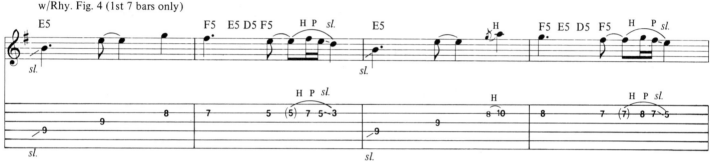

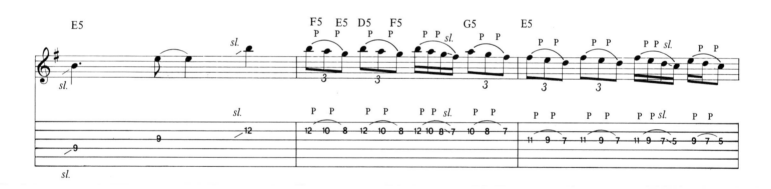

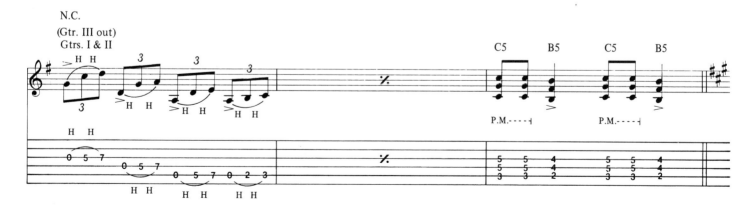

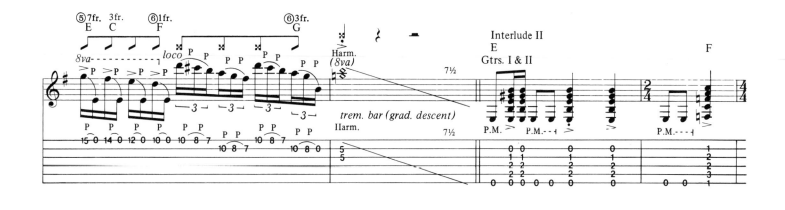

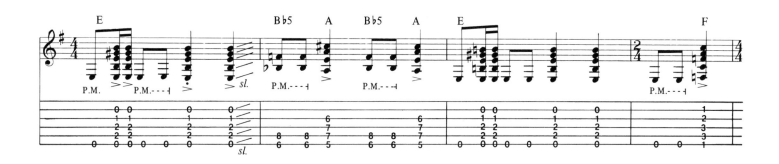

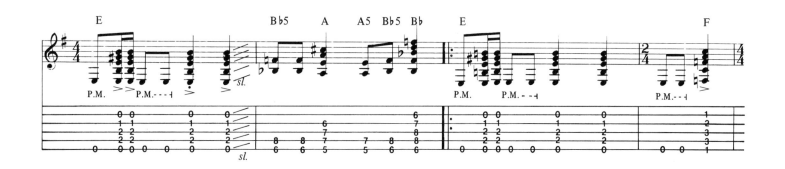

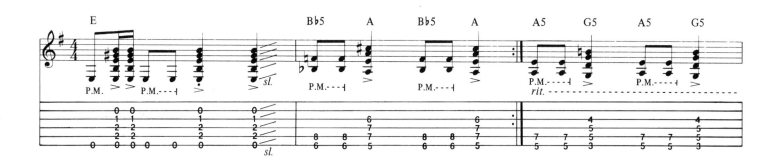

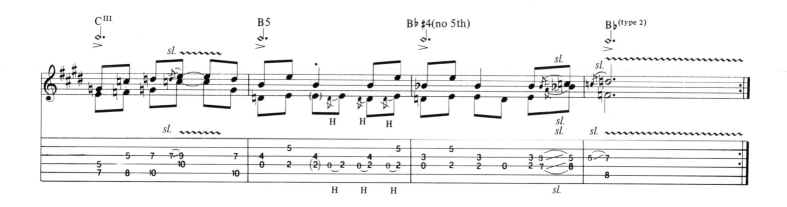

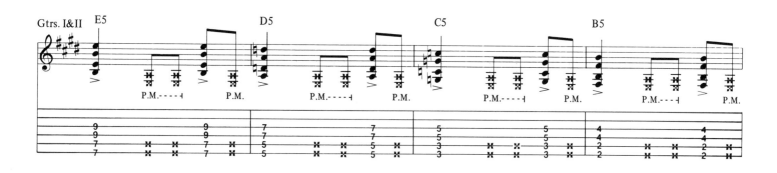

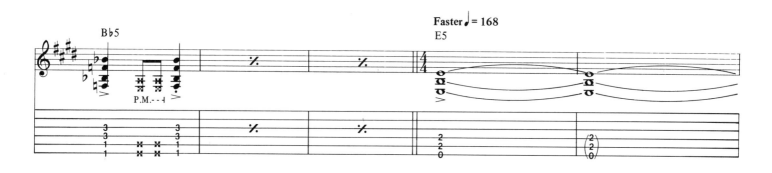

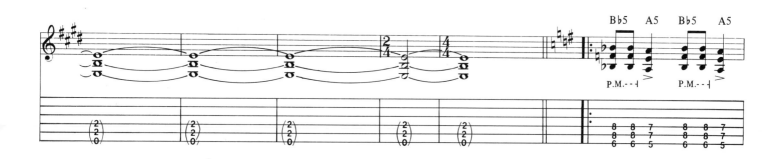

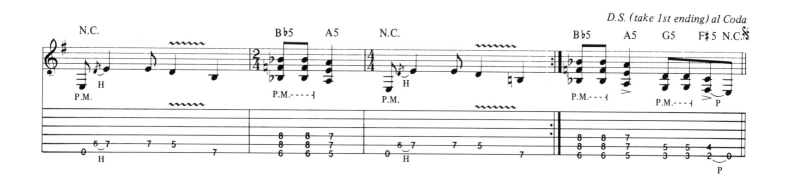

The Four Horsemen
from "Kill 'Em All"

Words and Music by
Lars Ulrich and Dave Mustaine

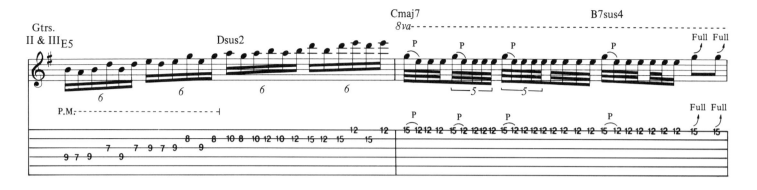

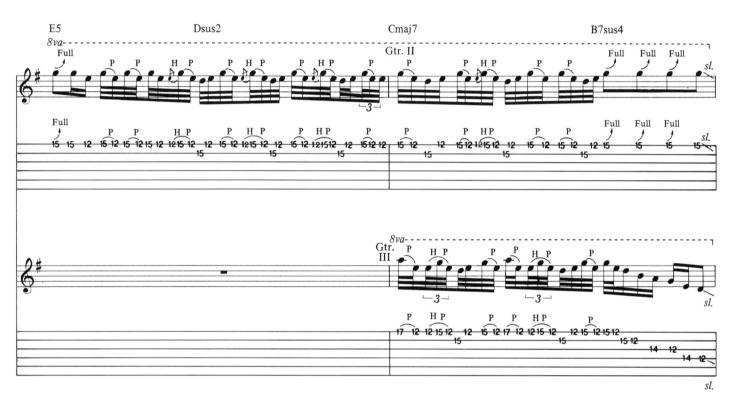

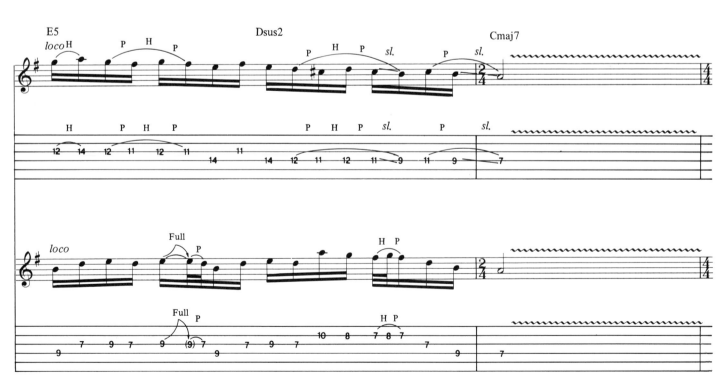

*Gtr. I: Depress bar after pull-off.
Gtr. II: Depress bar on first beat.
**Gtr. I indicated to right of slash in TAB.

*Can be approximated by steadily lowering
pitch of open low E string w/bar.

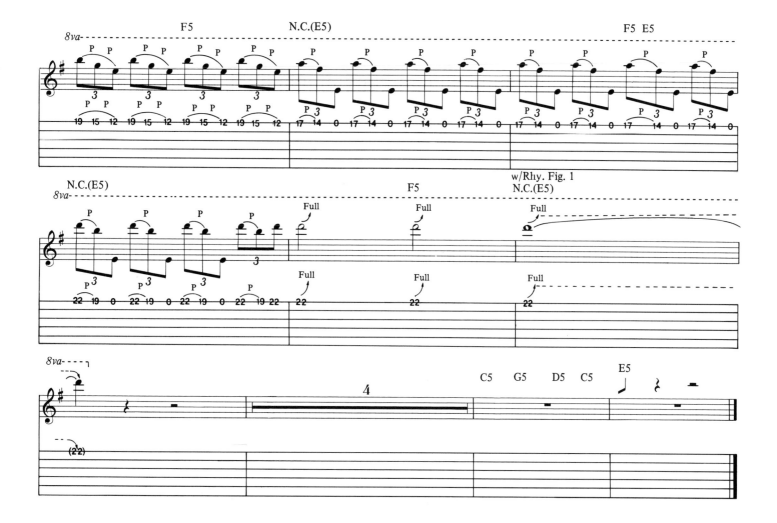

Additional Lyrics

2. You've been dying since the day you've been born.
   You know it's all been planned.
   The quartet of deliverance rides.
   A sinner once, a sinner twice,
   No need for confession now.
   'Cause now you've got the fight of your life. *(To Coda)*

3. So gather round young warriors now
   And saddle up your steeds.
   Killing scores with demon swords.
   Now is the death of doers of wrong.
   Swing the judgment hammer down.
   Safely inside armor, blood, guts and sweat. *(To Chorus)*

Welcome Home (Sanitarium)

from "Master Of Puppets"

Words and Music by
James Hetfield, Lars Ulrich
and Kirk Hammett

TABLATURE EXPLANATION

TABLATURE: A six-line staff that graphically represents the guitar fingerboard, with the top line indicating the highest sounding string (high E). By placing a number on the appropriate line, the string and fret of any note can be indicated. The number 0 represents an open string.

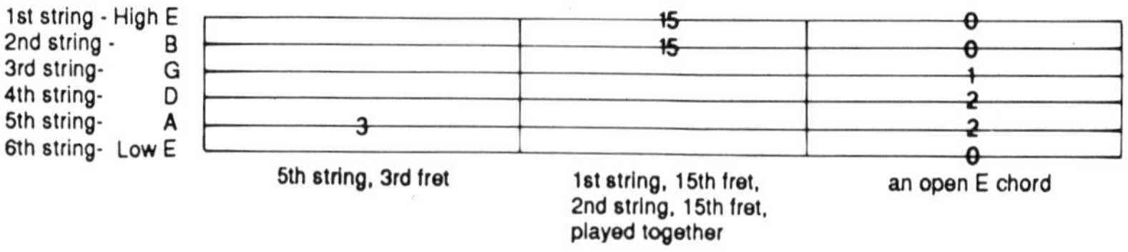
1st string - High E
2nd string - B
3rd string- G
4th string- D
5th string- A
6th string- Low E
5th string, 3rd fret
1st string, 15th fret, 2nd string, 15th fret, played together
an open E chord

Definitions for Special Guitar Notation

BEND: Strike the note and bend up ½ step (one fret).

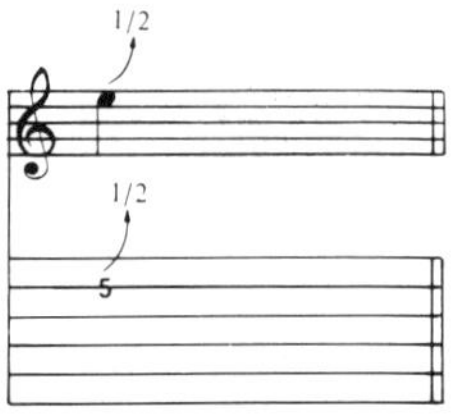
1/2
1/2

BEND: Strike the note and bend up a whole step (two frets).

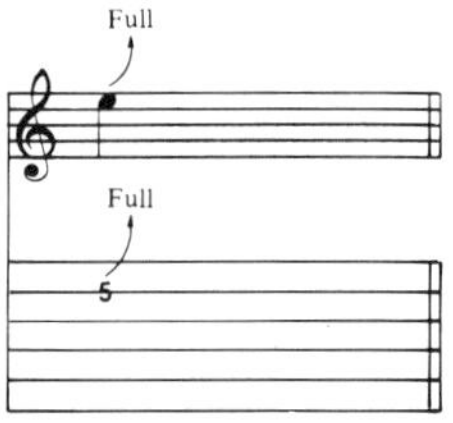
Full
Full

BEND AND RELEASE: Strike the note and bend up ½ (or whole) step, then release the bend back to the original note. All three notes are tied, only the first note is struck.

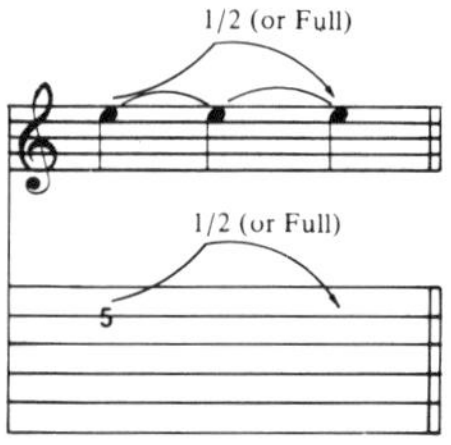
1/2 (or Full)
1/2 (or Full)

PRE-BEND: Bend the note up ½ (or whole) step, then strike it.

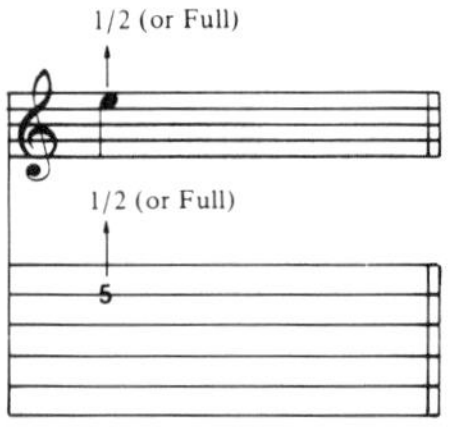
1/2 (or Full)
1/2 (or Full)

PRE-BEND AND RELEASE: Bend the note up ½ (or whole) step. Strike it and release the bend back to the original note.

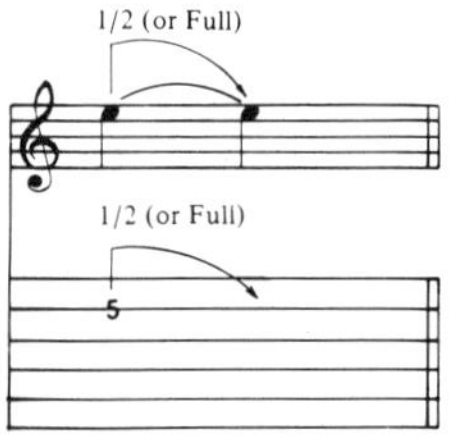
1/2 (or Full)
1/2 (or Full)

UNISON BEND: Strike the two notes simultaneously and bend the lower note up to the pitch of the higher.

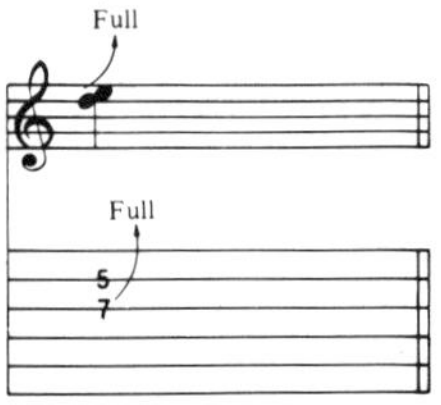
Full
Full

VIBRATO: The string is vibrated by rapidly bending and releasing the note with the left hand or tremolo bar.

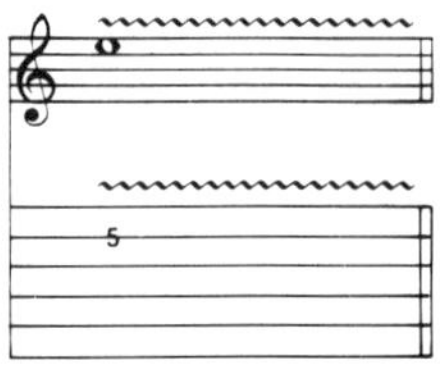

WIDE OR EXAGGERATED VIBRATO: The pitch is varied to a greater degree by vibrating with the left hand or tremolo bar.

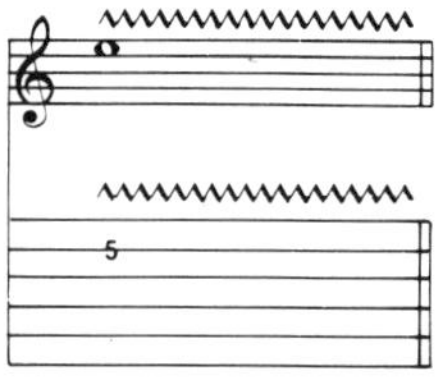

SLIDE: Strike the first note and then slide the same left-hand finger up or down to the second note. The second note is not struck.

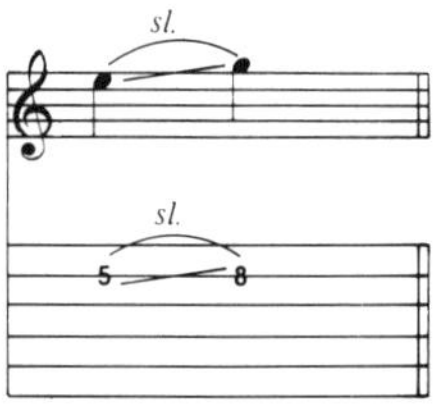
sl.
sl.

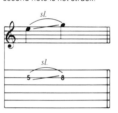

SLIDE: Same as above, except the second note is struck.

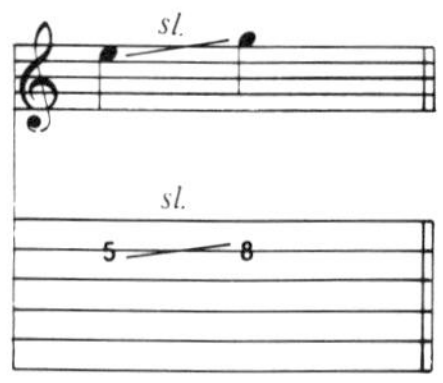
sl.
sl.

HAMMER-ON: Strike the first (lower) note, then sound the higher note with another finger by fretting it without picking.

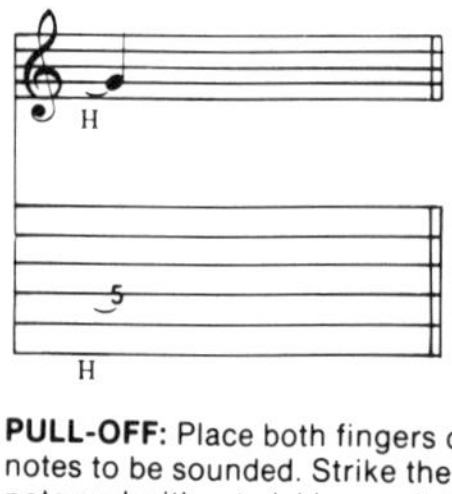
H
H

PULL-OFF: Place both fingers on the notes to be sounded. Strike the first note and without picking, pull the finger off to sound the second (lower) note.

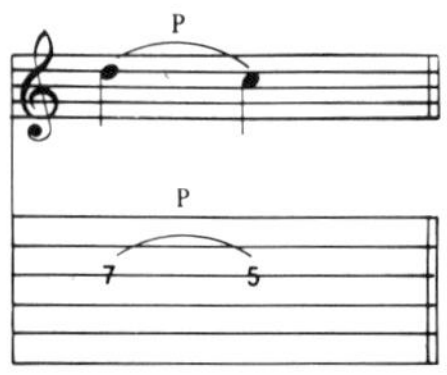
P
P

TRILL: Very rapidly alternate between the note indicated and the small note shown in parentheses by hammering on and pulling off.

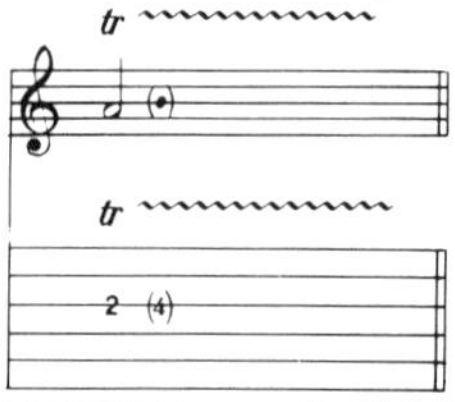
tr
tr

TAPPING: Hammer ("tap") the fret indicated with the right-hand index or middle finger and pull off to the note fretted by the left hand.

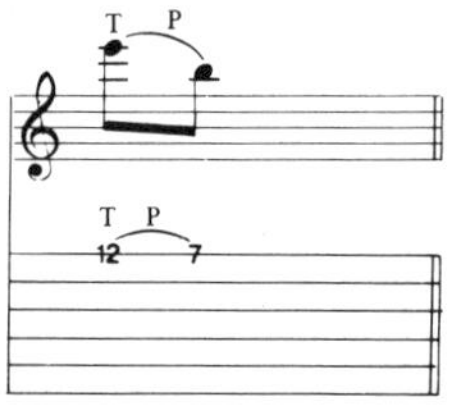
T P
T P

PICK SLIDE: The edge of the pick is rubbed down the length of the string producing a scratchy sound.

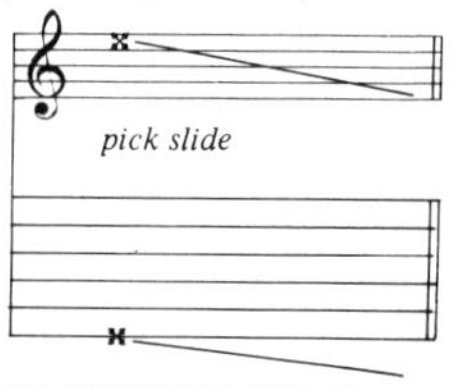
pick slide

TREMOLO PICKING: The note is picked as rapidly and continuously as possible.

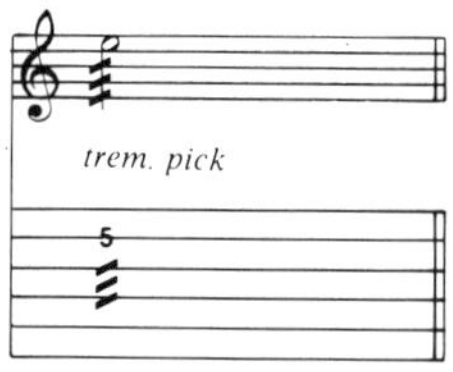
trem. pick

NATURAL HARMONIC: Strike the note while the left hand lightly touches the string over the fret indicated.

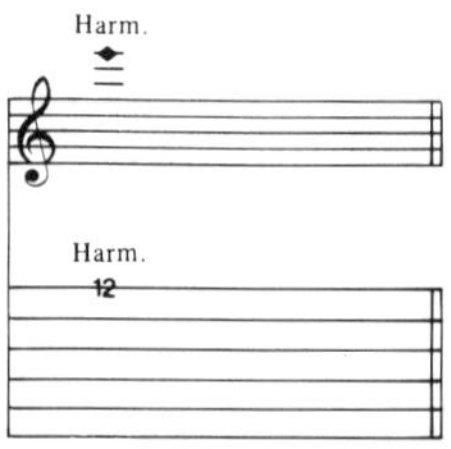
Harm.
Harm.

ARTIFICIAL HARMONIC: The note is fretted normally and a harmonic is produced by adding the edge of the thumb or the tip of the index finger of the right hand to the normal pick attack. High volume or distortion will allow for a greater variety of harmonics.

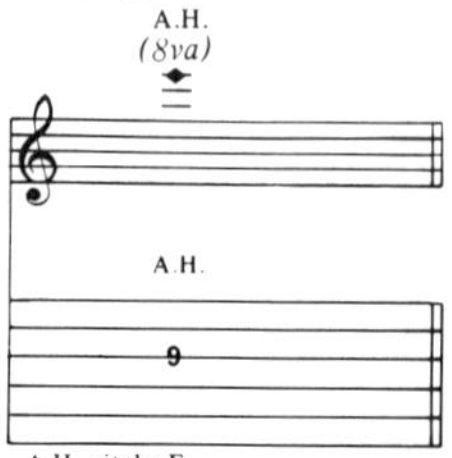
A.H.
(8va)
A.H.

A.H. pitch: E

TREMOLO BAR: The pitch of the note or chord is dropped a speci[fied] number of steps then returned to [the] original pitch.

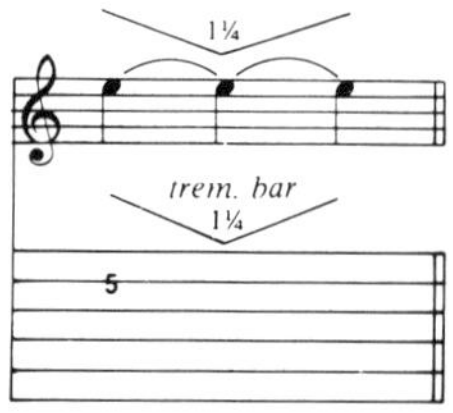
1¼
trem. bar
1¼

PALM MUTING: The note is par[tially] muted by the right hand lightly touching the string(s) just before [the] bridge.

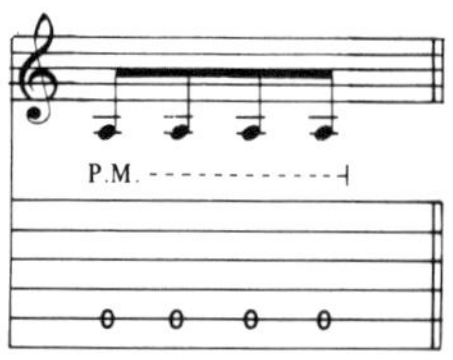
P.M.

MUFFLED STRINGS: A percuss[ive] sound is produced by laying the hand across the strings without depressing them and striking the[m] with the right hand.

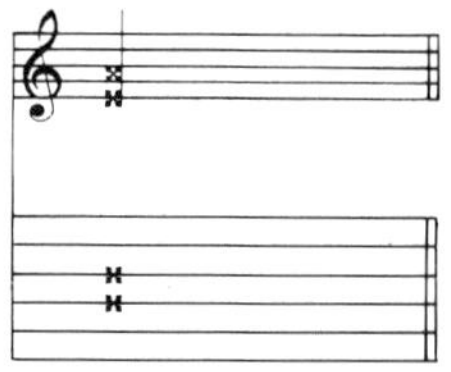

RHYTHM SLASHES: Strum cho[rds] in rhythm indicated. Use chord voicings found in the fingering diagrams at the top of the first p of the transcription.

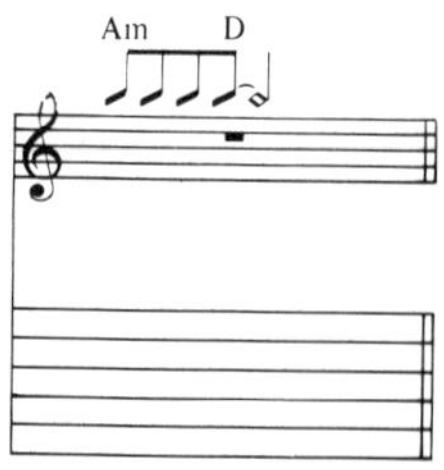
Am
D

RHYTHM SLASHES (SINGLE NOTES): Single notes can be indicated in rhythm slashes. The circled number above the note [n]ame indicates which string to play. W[hen] successive notes are played on [the] same string, only the fret numbe[rs] are given.

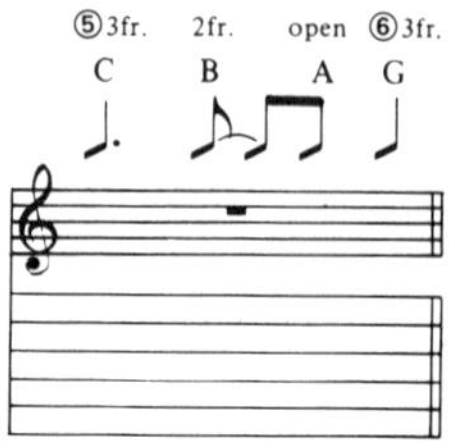
⑤3fr.
2fr.
open
⑥3fr.
C
B
A
G